I AM FREE

DAVID DELEVANTE
&
C. G. COOPER

Copyright © 2013 Cooper & Associates. All Rights Reserved

Authors: David Delevante, C. G. Cooper

Cover design by Humblenations.com

This is a work of fiction. Characters, names, locations and events are all products of the author's imagination. Any similarities to actual events or real persons are completely coincidental.

TABLE OF CONTENTS

Chapter 1:   The Job 5

Chapter 2:   James 14

Chapter 3:   The Opportunity 23

Chapter 4:   The Mistake 32

Chapter 5:   They Said No 42

Chapter 6:   The Event 49

Chapter 7:   A New Ally 62

Chapter 8:   Working The Business 69

Chapter 9:   My Name Is.... 75

CHAPTER 1
THE JOB

I gripped the steering wheel hard, white knuckles taking the pressure of the strain. One of the things I hated about driving to work was the near constant traffic. It turned what should've been a half hour commute into an hour and a half ordeal. Glancing at the clock, I noted that my wife was probably getting the twins on the school bus. I hadn't put them on the bus since their first day of kindergarten and they were now in third grade.

The thought made me angrier and angrier until I switched on the radio to hear an update about the bumper-to-bumper standstill on I-95.

"I hope you've brought a good book to read today, folks. Looks like you're in for a long drive in," informed the traffic reporter in a tone that grated my frayed nerves like metal on glass. He went on to describe not one but three accidents on my way in to work.

"I wish you were sitting here with me," I said to the faceless announcer through gritted teeth.

It hadn't always been this way, but the Washington, D.C./Northern Virginia area kept getting busier and busier. It didn't help that there was always road construction disrupting any semblance of a smooth traffic pattern.

I groaned as I picked up my cell phone to call the office. Our secretary answered after the third ring. I talked before she could utter a syllable. "Patty, it's Dan. I'm stuck in traffic on 95. Can you tell the boss that I'll be in as soon as I can?" I tried to add a little sugar to my tone knowing that if I didn't, Patty's legendary mood might jump through the phone.

"I'll tell him," Patty responded with her near seventy-year-old smoker's voice. "You're not the only one. See ya when I see ya."

The connection ended, and I breathed a sigh of relief. At least Patty was in decent spirits. That gave me a shred of hope for my morning, but there was still a pile of files waiting for me, and a conference call at ten.

+++

Forty-five minutes later, I pulled into the crowded parking lot of the five-story office building that housed my employer of almost twenty-years. As quickly as I could, I scooped up my briefcase and hustled to the door.

I somehow managed to finish my report before the conference call. Luckily, I'd taken the file home the night before and worked on it until midnight. Melissa, my wife, hated it when I brought work home. She said it took time away from her and the kids. That's why I'd taken to working after they'd gone to bed. It wasn't uncommon for me to work into the wee hours.

It should've been worth it. I made good money. We owned a nice home. The kids went to a great school. There wasn't much we needed, and yet…

By lunch, I was on my third cup of coffee. I told my assistant, Grant, a recent grad from George Mason University, to cut me off at five. I needed my fuel but I didn't need a heart attack. "Sure thing, Mr. -- I mean, Dan." It'd taken Grant almost a month to get to the point where he'd call me by my first name. "I just put your lunch on your desk. Is there anything else I can do?" Grant asked.

"Nope. Why don't you take some extra time for lunch? I won't need you until one." Grant had a new girlfriend from Accounting and I knew they liked to eat lunch together. It was the least I could do. He was a good kid and worked hard.

"Thanks!" He smiled and marched off to find his crush.

Taking a seat behind my desk, I looked at the pictures arrayed around my computer monitor. They were mostly of the kids, a boy and a girl, Jason and Jesse, at various points in their lives. There were the collages Melissa had made a year before. She loved that kind of stuff. So did I. It kept home as close as it could be. My favorite picture was the one I took of Melissa before we had kids. We'd taken a trip to the Bahamas and rented a sailboat for the day. I'd somehow caught the light perfectly as she'd sat in the bow looking out over the blue sea.

A pang of guilt hit my chest as I stared at the image. I'd always promised her that we'd go back to the same little resort and rent another sailboat. It hadn't happened. You know how it is. Work, and then kids. You get busy. Life gets in the way of, well, life.

I took a bite of my turkey and wheat sandwich. No mayo. I was on a diet kick again. Recent work overloads had kept me from getting back into my workout routine, at least that's what I told myself.

Everyday I allowed myself fifteen minutes during lunch to 'tune out' at work. I shut my work email and minimized the files I'd worked on earlier. As I devoured the rest of my sandwich I opened my personal email account and browsed the inbox.

Most of it was junk of some sort until I noticed a familiar name: James.

James was a good friend from college. He was one of those guys that everyone liked. James was outgoing, ruggedly handsome, and always up for an adventure. While I got an engineering degree, James took every fun liberal arts class he could. I hadn't talked to him in over a year. I was bad at that. It was usually him reaching out. The last I'd heard he'd move to Colorado, or was it Oregon?

I opened his email and read the short message:

Hey, Dan! I know it's last minute, but I'll be in town tonight. Wanted to see if I could

buy you dinner and catch up. Let me know!
- Jimbo

I was torn. While I really wanted to see James, Melissa needed help getting the kids to soccer and dance. I crossed my fingers and shot Melissa a text:

> *Hey, James is in town tonight and wants to buy me dinner. Would that be okay? Love you! -D*

I knew she'd be rolling her eyes, at least halfway. She liked James, too. The reply came through seconds later.

> *Sure. I'll work it out. Love you too* ☺

The worry crept in. Jeez, I loved my wife. I tried to shake off the guilt as I replied to James's email.

> *Would love to. I get off at five. Just tell me the time and place. – Dan*

I smiled and sat back in my ergonomic leather chair. It would be fun to see James again. I couldn't remember the last time we'd hung it out. It must've been…

My thoughts were cut off as my office phone rang. I sighed and picked it up.

NOTES

NOTES

CHAPTER 2

JAMES

Luckily I'd stashed an extra pair of jeans and a collared shirt in the company locker room. At 5pm, I rushed to get changed and then bolted out the door. The restaurant wasn't far, but you never knew how long it might take in traffic.

To my astonishment, traffic flowed smoothly and I got there ten minutes early. Stepping into the restaurant, I looked around for James. He was sitting at the bar, chatting with a pretty bartender.

I walked over and gave him an elbow in the back. James turned and hopped off the barstool. As was his custom, he gave me a crushing bear hug. James had a way of showing brotherly affection that I'd never picked up. Growing up, my family wasn't the touchy feely type. I'd gotten used to it with James and smiled as he put me down.

"What's going on, man?" asked James. "It's great to see you."

He had a way of making anyone feel welcome. I hadn't seen him in years and it still only seemed like a matter of days. We fell into our old routine as the hostess showed us to a booth.

"So how's the fam? How's Melissa doing?"

"Everybody's good. The twins are growing like weeds. Melissa said to say hello. She said you should've stayed over," I said.

"It was a last minute thing. I'm in town for the day on business. Flying back home tomorrow morning. Tell me about work. They still keeping you busy?"

I told him about my recent promotion and the mountain of work I'd taken on.

James cocked his head, measuring my expression. "You happy?"

To anyone else I probably would have lied and put on a brave face. With James, I found myself telling him the truth. "It's okay. I kinda feel like I'm missing my kids grow up."

He nodded solemnly. "Can you delegate some of your workload?"

I shrugged. "Maybe. I hadn't really thought about it."

"Same old Dan. Always taking on more than his share of the responsibility."

He was right. Doing the right thing was high on my To-Do list. I was good at what I did and people knew it. That led to me becoming sort of a task magnet. Things others couldn't do got thrown onto my pile.

"Do you have a Plan B?" asked James.

"What do you mean?"

"Have you ever thought about what you'd do if you didn't work for that company?"

"I don't know. I've been there so long."

"What about Melissa? What does she want?"

I was too embarrassed to say that I didn't know. Thankfully, before I could answer, the waiter arrived and took our orders.

James must have sensed my discomfort because he changed the subject and we swapped stories from our college glory days. By the time our food arrived, my stomach was sore from laughing.

We dug into the food as James rehashed stories I'd heard countless times. It didn't matter. He had a way of telling them that always kept them fresh. Somehow I managed to eat between chuckles.

"What about you?" I asked. "What are you up to these days?"

James smiled. "Life's really good."

I arched an eyebrow. It wasn't like James to hold back. I made a 'give it to me' gesture.

"Well, you know that I bounced around for a while. Made enough money to get by, but didn't like what I was doing. A few years ago I got involved with a network marketing company."

My heart stopped, and I almost dropped my fork. *Not James*, I thought. There'd been other friends who had made multi-level marketing pitches to me and Melissa over the years. Luckily, we'd never taken the plunge. How could this have happened?

James grinned. "I didn't tell you that I have cancer."

I coughed and tried to compose myself, preparing for the inevitable sales pitch. It never came.

"Relax. I'm here to catch up and that's it. I'm not here to sell you anything," James explained. My stomach untangled. "You asked what I was doing and I told you."

"It's just that…I'm sorry. I shouldn't have reacted that way. Let's just say that I've been lured into network marketing meetings before. It was never a pleasant experience. I shouldn't have assumed that you'd do the same thing. I'm sorry."

"Don't worry about it," said James. "Besides, I'm not ashamed of what I do. I make a very good living, travel as much as I want and get to help people every day."

He looked like the same James I'd known, but at that moment I realized something felt different. The last few times I'd seen him after college James seemed unsatisfied. This time was, well, different. James radiated a passion and confidence that drew me in. I was curious.

Before I could bite my tongue, the words blurted out of my mouth, "How much are you making?"

Without hesitating, he told me. My jaw could have hit the floor.

"You're kidding," I said, in what probably sounded like a gasp.

James chuckled without the slightest hint of arrogance. "Nope. I learned how to use the system and it worked."

All I could do was stare. How had James, a guy that I loved, but someone who'd never had much focus in life, go from making a modest middle-class living to becoming a multi-millionaire?

"Forget I said anything," James offered. "Let's get back to the old days."

I couldn't do it. Something in his words and his demeanor sparked a feeling deep in my gut, or was it my soul? I wanted what he had. Why couldn't I have what he had?

"How did you do it?" I asked, almost scared of the answer.

"You really wanna know?"

I nodded.

"Okay. It all started with…"

As I listened, James went on to describe his amazing journey. He told me about the network marketing company he'd joined and the colleague who'd introduced him to the opportunity. That colleague had never done anything with the business, but James had.

The rusty wheels of long-buried dreams started to crank slowly in my mind. *Could this be for me?*

PRACTICE

Make a list of dreams you put aside in order to have a 'normal' job. Did you ever want to be an artist, a musician or a doctor? Maybe you wanted to be a stay-at-home parent? Write down every dream you put on hold in order to have a 'normal' life.

NOTES

NOTES

CHAPTER 3
THE OPPORTUNITY

That night I couldn't sleep. Thoughts of my conversation with James swirled in my brain. It was almost too incredible to believe, but I did. He'd shown me pictures from recent speaking engagements and trips overseas to mentor other network marketers. A twinge of jealousy crept in as I flipped through the images. *Why hasn't he asked me to join?* I'd thought.

I knew why. My reaction to his network marketing declaration had said it all. I'd become closed off to opportunities outside my tiny little world, and James knew it.

Even after telling me his story, James never once offered an invitation. I respected him for that, but...it felt like I hadn't been invited to the club. It made me miserable. I wanted what he had.

The next morning, I left for work early, once again kissing a sleeping family goodbye. On the way to work I drove in silence, the usual radio chatter shuttered for the day.

There was a time when I'd dreamed of starting my own company and taking Melissa and the kids on vacation every month. Slowly the dream had vanished in a never-ending slog of work and a climb up the corporate ladder.

Suddenly everything came into stark focus, the daily grind, the days without seeing my kids, the months of not spending quality time with my wife. My losses were adding up as I crept closer to the office. Then, right there in the middle of the traffic jam, I picked up my phone and dialed James's number.

He picked up on the first ring. "Hey, Dan. What's up?" He sounded concerned. It was probably my look when we'd said goodbye the night before. Who knew how I'd come across.

"I just, um, wanted to say thanks again for dinner last night. It was great catching up," I said.

"No problem! Next time let's include the family."

"You got it. Hey, I was wondering, um…"

"Yeah?"

The words came out in a tumble, "I was wondering if you could tell me a little more about your network marketing thing."

"Tell you what, I'm sitting on the plane right now and we're about to take off. How about I give you a call when I land?"

"Okay. I'll talk to you then."

We said goodbye and ended the call. As I gazed out over the golden horizon, a glimmer of hope tingled through my body. The feeling spread into a giant smile, and a single tear of hope crept down my face. *Could this be the answer?*

+++

I could hardly concentrate on my work and spent most of the morning looking up James's company and explanations of network marketing on the Internet. The company stuff looked great, but the network marketing information was a mixed bag. It seemed that I wasn't the only person in the world who'd looked down on the industry.

I perused reviews and testimonials between phone calls and jotted down notes and questions to bring up with James. I wanted to be prepared.

Just after twelve my cell phone rang. It was James. I hurried to close my office door and answer the call.

"Hey," I said. "You get in okay?"

"Yeah. There was some guy snoring next to me, but my headphones took care of that. So you got a couple minutes to talk?"

"I do. I told my assistant that I was expecting an important phone call."

James laughed. "Good. I know you probably have a whole bunch of questions, but do you mind if I start with one of my own?"

"Of course not."

"Okay. What's your dream?"

It wasn't the question I was expecting and I struggled to find an answer I felt comfortable saying out loud. "I guess I want something similar to what you have."

"And what do you think I have?"

I searched for the right word. Money? Business? Passion?

"Freedom," I blurted.

"Freedom to do what?"

I could feel the walls coming down. I wanted to tell him what I wanted, but it had been so long since I'd verbalized any kind of a dream. How could I say it? Melissa didn't even know.

"I just, I want to have the freedom to take my kids to school, to eat lunch with them, to take my wife out to dinner, to go on vacation, to… to…" The rush of emotions cut me off. I couldn't remember the last time I'd let my feelings overwhelm me.

"Why can't you rearrange your work schedule to do those things?"

I thought about offering up the same list of excuses I always gave Melissa: too much responsibility at work, having to set the example, need to climb the corporate ladder, and on and on the list would go. Something inside cracked. I was tired of lying to myself.

"It's like you said at dinner, 'Same old Dan.' I don't know how to say no. I've been on this hamster wheel so long that I don't know anything different."

"Thanks for telling me," said James. "Does Melissa know?"

"I don't know," I answered truthfully. My wife rarely complained about our situation. Compared to a lot of people we knew, our life was perfect.

"Okay. Let me run through what I can do for you."

For the next fifteen minutes James explained why he'd left the "rat race" for something better. In general terms, he also told me about how he'd built his business from scratch. I hung on every word. I felt myself slamming the door open.

"I'm in." Those two little words felt powerful, inspiring.

"Okay. How about we sign you up now?"

I didn't hesitate. Raw unbridled energy coursed through my normally calm body. "Let's do it."

The process was easy. Within minutes I'd given him my vital information like address, phone number, etc., picked my initial order of products that I wanted to try personally, and that was it. I was officially an associate.

"You are now part of the team, my friend," said James, elation evident in his tone. "Ready to get to work?"

"Yeah."

Next, he delivered my plan.

"If you're serious, here's what I want you to do next. You have two homework assignments. First, in three to four sentences, describe your perfect life. Be as descriptive as you can. I want to picture you living that life. Second, jot down twelve people that you'd like to share the business with."

I scribbled what he was saying on my always-handy yellow legal pad.

"Is that all?" I asked, ready to jump in with both feet.

"That's it. Do those two things and let's talk again tomorrow."

PRACTICE

Step 1: In three to four sentences, describe your perfect life. Be as descriptive as possible. Would you sleep until noon, take your kids to school, snorkel before breakfast, or live in the mountains? Imagine what it would look, sound and taste like. Make it vivid.

Step 2: Make a list of 12 people you can contact about your business opportunity. Do not discriminate! Just write down the first 12 that come to mind.

NOTES

NOTES

CHAPTER 4
THE MISTAKE

It took me most of the night to whittle my perfect life down to four sentences. Once I opened the hatch, my dreams flooded out. It surprised me. I hadn't realized how much my life had drifted. Others might have thought that I led the ideal life, but all I could think about was what I wasn't doing.

Don't get me wrong. It's not that I wasn't grateful. I had a good job with a great company. It's just that I didn't own my time. I'd traded it for the opportunity to rise to the top. Where would it end?

Once I got my perfect life in writing, I moved on to listing the twelve people I wanted to contact first. My brother came to mind. I wrote his name on the list. A friend from church. I wrote his name on the list. In less than five minutes my twelve slots were full.

I was too jazzed to sleep. Instead of joining my peacefully sleeping wife, I cracked open my laptop. An idea came to mind.

Before I knew it, I'd drafted a five-paragraph synopsis of the network marketing company I'd joined earlier in the day and my goals for the future. My analytical mind happily reviewed the expertly drafted message. I pressed SEND and the email shot into cyberspace, bound for the twelve people on my list.

My mission accomplished, I closed my laptop, turned off the bedside lamp and lay down with a contented grunt. I drifted off to sleep on thoughts of gently lapping waves and my wife and kids playing in the surf.

+++

The next day I called James at the appointed time. Before he got a word in, I told him everything that I'd done. I just had to get my enthusiasm out. It was so unlike me. I wanted him to tell me how great I'd done.

It didn't quite happen that way.

"Okay," started James. "Let me first say that I love the description of your perfect life. I could feel the emotion you put into it. I'd say you also did a good job listing your first twelve contacts, but here's the thing, did I tell you to email them?" There wasn't a hint of disappointment or criticism in his voice, and yet, I knew I'd screwed up. James waited patiently for my response as I stumbled to find the words to explain.

"I just, um, I thought I'd get the ball rolling," I said.

James chuckled. "I understand. I could see you were excited. I know emails work in your current line of work, but network marketing is better when it's face-to-face or at least over the phone. Let me ask you something. What would you have done if I'd sent you an email telling you about my business?"

I exhaled and my head dropped. "I probably wouldn't have wanted to talk about it."

"That's the thing about network marketing. Most times the dream is more important. You wanted to know about what I was doing because you saw that I was living my dream."

His explanation made stark sense. If James had approached me about joining his business I probably would have politely brushed him off. As the error of my actions took hold, my stomach clenched. Had I just killed my chances with the first twelve people on my list?

"How do I fix this?" I said, desperation seeping into my tone.

"Do you trust me?"

"I, uh, of course."

"Do you trust me when I say that I wouldn't tell you to do anything that I haven't already done a thousand times?" His soothing voice brought my heart rate back within normal parameters.

"I trust you."

"Good. Here's what we're going to do. I'm going to teach you how to invite."

"Invite what?" I asked.

"Invite the twelve people on your list."

I groaned. "We're not gonna trick them into going to some hotel meeting are we?"

"Dan, do you honestly believe that I would ask you to do that?"

I wasn't sure. I'd been duped into those meetings before. "I guess not."

"Remember, trust me. Now, I don't want you to sell anything. That's my job. I'll be with you every step of the way. The only thing I want you to learn is how to invite people to talk to me."

I didn't mind not having to sell, but this went against everything I'd ever heard about network marketing. "Shouldn't I tell them about the products and stuff like that?" I already had a printout I'd constructed with the highlights of each.

"The products are important, but the dream is even more important. I learned a long time ago that finding out whether a person has a half-buried dream is way more crucial than seeing if they like the product. Our products, by the way, are some of the best on the planet, but what I'm selling is a system that gets people like you and me closer to our dreams. Make sense?"

"I think so," I answered, even though I wasn't sure if I really did get it.

"Let me see if this explains it better. When I first started my business, I was all about selling the products. I talked about them to everyone who would listen. It got to a point to where I felt like a used car salesman, and very few people like those guys. I was fortunate enough to meet a high-ranking partner who took me under his wing. He taught me that the selling of products and services is merely the vehicle we use to attain our dreams. People need to get the Why. The How comes later."

It was a new thought process for me. In my world, it was all about learning a system and service inside and out first. You couldn't go to a potential client without that experience and knowledge. What James was saying was as foreign to me as a trip to Saturn aboard an alien spaceship.

"So you're saying that we find the need?" I asked.

"Exactly! But remember, that's my job. Just keep thinking back to when we had dinner. You were open to the idea of network marketing because of my journey and because you have a powerful dream. It was buried, but it was there. You want to spend time with your family and live a fuller life. Who could argue with that?"

He was right. It was going to be hard to get out of my own head. Truth be told, I had a tendency to be a bit obsessive compulsive about knowing a business inside and out. From what James was saying, I would need to put that aside. The dream was more important.

"Okay. Teach me how to invite."

"We'll start with what's in it for them. That's what your prospects want to know. How is this opportunity going to help them? You'll need to know a little bit about their circumstances, of course. Next you need to tell them what your vision is."

"Isn't that a little premature? I mean, I just signed up," I said.

"Buddy, it doesn't matter if you have ten minutes or ten years in this business. Even if you haven't attained your desired end state, you still need to vocalize it. Here, let me give you an example of what you might say."

My pen and paper were ready.

James continued, "I'm calling my buddy Lou who I know a bit about. Here's what I would say, 'Lou, I know you've mentioned that your wife would really like to be at home with the kids instead of working. I have my own business in addition to my day job. My goal is to be able to leave my day job within the next five years. I don't know if this is a perfect fit for you and your wife, but it could be a way to get her home. Would it be okay if I have my partner James give you a quick five-minute call?' That's it!"

Days earlier I would have run for the hills, but now, something had changed. I could picture my vision. It was palpable. I could almost taste it. So off I went. Instead of worrying about looking like a fool to the twelve I'd already emailed the night before, I focused on my perfect life.

PRACTICE

Network marketing is all about inviting, not information. Oftentimes, less is more. As human beings, we tend to data dump on people when we're excited. It's important to get our heads out of the conversation and let our hearts do the talking.

By now you've paid for your distributorship. You're in business.

Next, get with your mentor. Have them help you come up with a script to use. They should be able to find a way of inviting that makes you feel comfortable. Remember, your only job is to invite your contacts to talk to your mentor. Do not try to sell!

NOTES

NOTES

CHAPTER 5
THEY SAID NO

During my lunch break I summoned the courage to sit down in my car and call my list of twelve. I got to three.

The first one didn't answer. I did not leave a message. The second, my cousin in California, said no. The third, a friend from the YMCA, said he would be out of town for the next week and that I should call him back then. I took that as a polite no.

My hand was shaking as I put the phone down. Three phone calls and nothing. In my head I thought it was going to be easier. Once again my nerves raged at the thought of making another call. Instead of dwelling on the disappointment, I took James's advice and called him.

I quickly gave him a rundown of what had happened.

"You told them why you were doing it and went by the script?" he asked.

"I did."

"Then you have nothing to worry about."

"But none of them said yes."

"Dan, part of this is about getting you out of your comfort zone. Are you there yet?"

I actually laughed. "Of course I am."

"Good. Let me let you in on another little secret." I pressed my ear into the phone, ready for the magic pill that would put me back on the path to my dreams. "You are going to hear *no* a lot."

I waited for him to continue. "And?" I asked.

"That's it."

"But…"

"Look, hearing no, especially from your friends and family, isn't fun. That's why it's so important to have a powerful dream. Without it you won't make even the first twelve phone calls. Only one person in my family became part of my team and that's my mom! Do you know how many aunts, uncles and cousins I have?"

"No."

"A lot! I know it's easier said than done, but those of us that succeed in this business just get used to hearing no. I can't tell you when it gets easier. Sometimes it takes a long time. The important thing is to keep speaking your vision and pressing forward."

"Should I even have my family on the list?" I asked.

"Yes. Years from now, when you've achieved everything you ever wanted, you do not want to look back and regret not offering it to them. I'll save you the suspense and tell you that most of them will probably say no."

"Why?" Family members made up half of my list of twelve!

"It's a strange thing. Family is great. They're with us through thick and thin. I think that's why they don't believe us sometimes. They think they know us too well. I swear in their heads they're thinking, "Oh, I *know* James and he'll do well, but not *that* well."

"That sounds pretty cynical," I frowned, not wanting to believe that my own family might turn against me.

"It's the truth. I have a friend who writes books. He sells a lot of them. He's built a multi-million dollar brand all by himself. To this day, despite the house, wonderful vacations, and no debt, his family still thinks it's some kind of trick. They don't believe it. It's the same with most of my family. Sure, my mom loves it and gushes about me whenever she can, but the rest of them tend to give me that funny look. I swear one of my uncles thinks I sell drugs."

That made me laugh. "You're kidding."

"Nope. Something happens when you're close to fame or fortune. It's like you don't want to believe it. They love you and try to protect you. More importantly, they want to protect the relationship they have with you. It's comfortable right now. They don't want to disturb the status quo. If you change those circumstances by getting super successful or taking off on an adventure it scares them. People don't do well with fear. Either way, I'm not a psychologist, just a guy who's seen it a few times."

I still couldn't believe that James's family treated him that way. He'd always been humble and giving even when he hadn't had a dollar in his pocket. It amazed me that people could be so blind.

"So I should still call my original list of twelve?"

"Yes. But, don't forget that you're already a quarter of the way done!"

Optimism. It was a trait I'd always admired in James and would grow to respect even more in the coming months.

PRACTICE

This is one of the hardest lessons to learn in any business, but for some reason it's even harder with network marketing.

Understand right here and now that you will hear 'no' more than you'd probably like. It's a byproduct of being in business. It's not for everyone.

But remember, at this point you aren't selling anything. You are merely offering them a peek into your dream. Internalize your perfect life and refer to it when a 'no' hits you the wrong way.

Take out a paper and write the following sentence:

Every NO gets me closer to a YES.

NOTES

NOTES

CHAPTER 6
THE EVENT

Mustering every ounce of courage in my body, I finished making my phone calls. I stuck to the script and tried to sound as upbeat as I could. I pictured James sitting beside me, nodding his head as I recited my invitation time and again.

I didn't stop until I'd called the last name on my list. When I hung up with my buddy Kevin, I slumped back in the leather seat and closed my eyes. I'd done it.

The midday sun streamed in as I opened my eyes and looked down at my call sheet. Here was the final tally: six no's, two no answers, one 'maybe later' and three said YES. The three who said yes were waiting for James to call. I wasted no time texting him (he was on another flight to someplace) the information for each yes. Here's what I sent:

- *Prospect: Neil*
- *needs money for kids' college*
- *scared of being laid off at work*
- *married with 3 kids*
- *very health conscious*
- *asked if it was sales*

I sent three such texts and then breathed a sigh of relief.

Climbing out of my car, I reentered, exhausted yet triumphant, our corporate offices. Somehow the rest of the day flew by with me in the middle of a whirlwind of productivity.

+++

On the way home James texted me back and told me that he would call my three contacts later that night. He also added:

> *A friend of mine is running an invite-only company training event tomorrow night. How would you like to take Melissa so she can see what you're up to? Let me know and I can tell them to expect you.*

My chest tightened. I hadn't told Melissa yet. Who knew what she'd say.

I texted James back: *Let me talk to M. I'll let you know.*

+++

I was quiet all through dinner that night. Instead of making eye contact with my wife, I focused on taking bite after bite.

"Are you okay, honey?" Melissa asked, not nagging, just concerned.

"What? Oh yeah. Sorry, just thinking about work."

She didn't look convinced, but let it go. Melissa was good like that.

After dinner, I ignored my laptop and spent time with the kids. We played a game of speed Monopoly. I lost big time. Melissa watched from the couch, a wonderful smile never leaving her beautiful face. By the end of the game, I was sandwiched by the twins, each jockeying over who could sit on my lap despite their age.

After tucking the kids in, Melissa and I headed to our room to get ready for bed. It was early for me. I was tired and it probably showed.

Melissa caught me with a surprise hug as I was brushing my teeth.

I smiled. "What was that for?"

She looked up at me with those eyes that had sucked me in the first time we'd met. "It was really nice of you to play with the kids after dinner. Did you see how much they loved it?"

"Yeah." I put my toothbrush down and held her in my arms. "Have I really been that bad?"

I could feel her shrug in my embrace. "You've just been really busy, honey. The kids and I understand."

I gently grabbed her by the shoulders and held her to arm's length. "I need to tell you something."

I quickly explained the details I'd failed to provide from my dinner with James along with the fact that I'd officially joined a network marketing company.

"What do you think?" I asked, breathless, hoping beyond hope that she'd hug me again.

Melissa sat in what I can only describe as shocked silence.

"I don't understand," she said, finally. "I thought you loved work."

My mind fumbled to find a response. I'd never told her my deepest feelings. I'd always thought that if I told her how work had become a daily battle that she'd get scared. That was the last thing I wanted. We avoided conflict.

"There's a training event tomorrow night. How about you come with me? That should clear things up." I forced a smile, hoping she would return it. Instead, Melissa nodded, got up, and silently got ready for bed.

I knew I was in trouble.

+++

The next day, I was a nervous wreck. I hadn't slept well and Melissa had barely said two words to me.

I told my assistant that I did not want to be bothered. Enclosed in my office, I did what I'd always done: work. Working right through lunch (I didn't have an appetite either), I plowed through the neatly stacked presentations and clipped away at my email inbox.

My internal alarm told me it was five o'clock without having to look at my watch. Melissa had texted earlier to say that she'd gotten a babysitter for the twins and that she'd be waiting to be picked up when I got home.

Rushing to my car, the impending confrontation looming ominously over my head, I prepared for the worst.

+++

Melissa gave me a quick kiss on the cheek as she climbed into the car. I waved to the kids as we pulled out of the drive. We'd be cutting it close.

Thirty minutes later, we parked in front of the address James had given me. It was a modest two-story brick home with a well-manicured lawn.

We walked to the front door hand-in-hand, she by habit, me wanting to make sure she wouldn't run. A woman opened the door just as we stepped up onto the landing.

"Hi! You must be Dan and Melissa. I'm Janet."

We shook hands with our host and followed her into the neatly furnished home. Melissa seemed to be taking it all in with her impeccable sense of fashion. She sometimes helped an interior designer friend on larger jobs. I'd told her on more than one occasion that she should open her own design business. Melissa always laughed at the idea and said she didn't have time.

There were twelve men and women mingling in the living room when we entered. They stopped talking as we came in.

"Guys, I want to introduce you to Dan and Melissa. They're old friends of James, whom you all know," Janet announced.

One by one the others stepped up to introduce themselves. I kept glancing at Melissa to read her facial expression. She was more comfortable at social gatherings, and laughed and chatted effortlessly. I, on the other hand, could feel the sweat trickling down my back.

James hadn't fully explained what the meeting was all about other than to say that it was an elite training group of sorts. Apparently we were the final guests to arrive, and once we'd met everyone in the room, we all took seats on couches and hastily gathered dining room chairs.

I'm not sure what I had expected, maybe a board room, but I settled in, held Melissa's hand and prayed the night would go well.

Our host, Janet, stood up and spoke. "Thanks for coming, everyone. Once again, welcome to the business, Dan and Melissa. You both come very highly recommended and we're happy to have you. Now, why don't we start by going around the room and telling our guests a little bit about ourselves? I'll start. I got into network marketing ten years ago. Initially, I signed up for the products because I liked them. That's all I did for five years. I was an attorney so I thought that finding the time to do both was impossible. Well, by my fifth year in the business I was making a couple thousand dollars every month just by telling my friends about the products. That's all I did. I never actively recruited, although some people signed up when they saw the opportunity.

"That same year my husband and I decided to separate. We were both attorneys and never saw each other. Still great friends, we'd simply lost our passion for one another. It was tough. We'd been together since college. Long story short, I decided to take a vacation and clear my head. Right before I left, I got one of the monthly mailers from our company. It said there would be a regional training event in Las Vegas the very same weekend I was going to Los Angeles. On a whim I registered, changed my flight, and flew to Vegas. That weekend changed my life. I met network marketers that were actually working the business. They came from all walks of life and were wonderfully supportive. I cried that first night in the arms of a total stranger. I wasn't the only one.

"Lying in bed that night, I realized I wanted something more. I was tired of working ninety-hour weeks just to make partner at the firm. I decided to change my course. In front of all those people, I declared my intention to work my network marketing business until I could leave my job. It took me eighteen months."

Everyone in the room clapped and hooted as Janet took her seat. Similar stories were recounted as the focus shifted around the room.

There was the salesman who'd left his company of thirty years and the recent college grad who hadn't even thought about getting a real job. A doctor stood up and told us how he'd lost his love for medicine before graduating from medical school, but had continued on for years without another option until he'd been introduced to network marketing by a patient. He'd sold his medical practice four years later. On and on the stories went. I felt myself being swept up into the passion of the group.

Three quarters of those assembled ran their network marketing businesses full time. The rest were close to being able to do the same.

Melissa's face remained stoic. I couldn't figure out what she was thinking.

Once the woman sitting next to me finished her story, Janet said, "Dan, I know you're new to network marketing, but we'd love for you to stand up and tell us why you joined."

My stomach tightened reflexively. I hated public speaking. Face flushed, I stood to give my story. Maybe it was because everyone else had been so open and honest about their stories that my internal wall of distrust dissolved.

"As you know, my name is Dan. My old college buddy James introduced me to the business after I pestered him about it." Everyone except Melissa chuckled. "I've got a good job and great family." I smiled down at my wife and paused. It was something in her eyes that told me that for once in my life I had to open up. "I… from the outside everything looks great. Heck, Melissa does all the hard work with the kids. I just…I never get to see them. I want to see them and spend time with them. I want to be able take my wife out to lunch and dinner. I want to be able to take the kids to Disneyworld. I want…" I gritted my teeth, fighting back the tears that I did not want to shed in front of strangers. They came anyway. "There's so much I want to do." I paused again as a thought seared into my subconscious. I latched on and road it. Looking down at my wife with confidence I hadn't felt in years, I said, "I want to quit my job in two years."

PRACTICE

We all have different reasons for starting in network marketing. Some people just want a little extra spending money. Others want the freedom to make a steady income without a nine-to-five job.

What's your goal? Write down where you want to be in two, five and ten years.

NOTES

NOTES

CHAPTER 7
A NEW ALLY

I don't remember what happened the rest of the night. What I'd said out loud kept playing over and over in my head. I'd never done anything like that. Melissa didn't say a thing until we got back in the car and started for home.

"Did you really mean what you said?" Melissa asked.

Keeping my eyes on the darkened road, I nodded and said, "Yeah."

"I didn't know you felt that way."

"I…I do."

"I'm glad," she said.

Her words shot a bolt of hope through my aching soul.

"What?"

"I said I'm glad. I want you to spend more time with us. I want all the things you want."

Tears, once again, came unbidden. I pulled the car into a school parking lot and turned to face my wife.

"I'm so sorry I never told you. I just... I didn't want you to worry," I said.

Her hand stroked the side of my face. I noticed the streaks of tears running from her beautiful eyes. "It's okay, honey. At least now we're on the same page."

She kissed me tenderly as we cried in unexpected relief.

+++

The next morning, on the way to work, I called James and told him about what had happened.

"I'm really happy for you, buddy," he said. "I can't tell you how important it is to have your wife onboard. I've seen a lot of potential success stories derailed without it."

"Thanks for introducing us to Janet and the rest of the group. They were awesome."

"Yeah. Me and Janet go back a few years. She's come a long way. Now she can't be stopped. She'll be great to have nearby when I can't be there. You ready to build your business?"

"I am."

"Okay. Like I promised, I talked to the three prospects you sent me. Out of those three it looks like we have the first member of your team!"

I almost dropped my phone in surprise. "When were you planning on telling me?" I said in frenzied frustration, although a grin showed how I really felt.

"I just got the call. Let's talk about what we need to do next."

I listened as he explained the process of enrolling a new associate. James said that for the first few months he would do all the recruiting for me and train my new people. My only job was to invite my prospects to talk to James.

"Do you think Melissa might want to help?" James asked.

"I don't know. I'll ask her tonight."

+++

That night I gave Melissa a rundown of everything James had told me. As was her way, she took notes as I spoke and nodded her comprehension.

When I was finished, she asked, "Can I help?"

I smiled. "Of course!"

"Okay, here's who I think you should contact first…" By the time Melissa was done writing, we had a list of fifty names.

"You sure you haven't done this before?" I asked with a grin.

It was Melissa's turn to smile. "I want this for you…for us."

That's all she had to say. With Melissa on my side, stepping out of my comfort zone and holding myself accountable to making invites got infinitely easier.

PRACTICE

It is vitally important to have an ally in your corner. Usually that means having your husband, wife or significant other on your side.

If you haven't done so already, it's time to share your dream with them. Tell them WHY you're doing network marketing. Let them know that's it's not just about you. Paint a picture for them that will explain your goals.

Having that person with you not only gives you added courage to confront the challenges of growing your business, it also holds you accountable to someone other than yourself. Let them know how much their support means to you. It can be the deciding factor between winning and losing.

NOTES

NOTES

CHAPTER 8
WORKING THE BUSINESS

Over the next three months I did everything James said. I set aside time to make my calls every day. I heard plenty of no's, but the yes's trickled in, too.

True to his word, James took care of the enrollment of my budding organization and trained them to do the same. It wasn't until I'd been in the business for close to ninety days that I even thought about giving a presentation.

Some days were easier than others. Some days it took a little prodding from Melissa to get off my rear and make my daily phone calls. I'd grumble for a second and then get to it. It always felt better when I was done.

Because I was so busy with my day job, I had to be systematic about my prospecting. I didn't have time to network in local groups. I couldn't go out for coffee or lunch. I stuck to a strict routine.

It got to the point where my day didn't feel complete unless I'd made my prospecting phone calls.

At least once a week I talked to James or Janet about my progress. It was great to have the big dogs on my side. I felt privileged until I realized they did that with any new partner who was serious about growing their network marketing business. I asked James about it one day, and he explained the rationale. "If I let you stick to inviting and I do the heavy lifting for a while, pretty soon you grow. The more I motivate your team, the more my organization grows. We're all in this together, so it behooves us top associates to lend our skills to you."

It was a lot more giving than I was used to. At my day job, each department pretty much fended for itself. It wasn't that we didn't all contribute, but we were so focused on our individual missions that taking on more responsibility didn't make sense.

There were more benefits to network marketing that emerged as I improved and grew my business. I came from a corporate culture that was big on personal achievement and growth. Network marketing totally blew that away. I met associates that read a new book every week and attended workshops and retreats to improve themselves mentally, spiritually and relationally.

The other benefit that made its mark on both Melissa and me was the new relationships we made. Our network marketing company was full of fun, smart and hard-working associates who never hesitated to lend a helping hand.

We found other couples with kids and went out to dinner, had bonfires and met at parks to play and hang out. Other times we went out for a nice dinner without the kids, and enjoyed the company of new friends. It had all happened so fast.

By the time I'd hit my 100th day in network marketing, I'd managed to personally sponsor fifteen people into my organization. They, in turn, and with James's help, had grown my team to sixty-eight partners. I couldn't believe it. I'd made forward progress, even picking up a couple bonuses from the company along the way. The money wasn't rolling in yet, but I knew my path and I knew my destination. I would make it.

PRACTICE

Your business will not grow itself. It's time to get out there and do the work. Write down specific tasks you will do each and every day to grow your business. If you're having trouble, get your mentor to help you.

It takes twenty-seven days to form a new habit. You now have a new habit to form, and it's called 'inviting.'

Keep your task list handy and look at it daily. Put it in your calendar. Set reminders so you don't forget. Do not go to bed until your tasks are completed.

NOTES

NOTES

CHAPTER 9
MY NAME IS...

It's been two years since I told my wife about my network marketing venture. There have been ups and downs. I've screwed up plenty, but through it all I've kept my head down and pressed ahead.

I wasn't used to asking for help or leaning on others. At my day job, Dan was the rock. You came to me if you needed help. I've learned that network marketing is a team sport. James has definitely been the biggest influence on my business, but there have been many more who have given a helping hand whether through encouragement, training or prayers.

By doing what James told me, I also learned how to be a leader. In network marketing it's all about leading by example. I guess that's true for most things, and yet it feels even more important when you're trying to lead a volunteer army.

I've seen great people come and go. Some have lost their passion. Others have had it taken from them either by a bitter spouse or an unsupportive host of friends. It's hard to watch, but it's part of any organization. Even better, I've also seen people who were teachable, that stuck to it and had their lives transformed for the better with improved finances, blossoming relationships, healthier lifestyles and an awesome quality of life. It makes me smile just thinking about it.

When you put your heart and soul into something, you change in ways you might never have imagined. Through this experience I've become a better husband, a better father and a better friend.

Do you want to know something funny? I never realized how important it was to listen. Did you know that most times you do more good by listening than by speaking? Sometimes when I'm prospecting, all I do is ask an open-ended question and then shut my mouth. You'd be amazed at what people, even complete strangers, will tell you. They'll tell you their hopes and dreams while you just sit there and smile.

That's what I love. I'm in the business of helping my friends achieve their hopes and dreams. Not everyone will get there and that's okay.

Here are some other things I've learned along the way:

- *Purge negativity from your life. It's like a contagious cancer that can eat away at even the most optimistic person and their relationships.*
- *Always keep an open mind. A closed mind attracts nothing.*
- *There is no demographic for the perfect network marketer.*
- *The superstar in your organization will probably be someone you've never met.*
- *Don't judge a book by its cover. People will surprise you mostly for the good, but sometimes for the bad.*
- *Smile. Its power will surprise you.*
- *Tell your story. It's the most powerful tool you have.*
- *Don't dump all the details on prospects. Pay plans and product specifications have their place, but nothing can top a beautiful dream.*

Right now I'm waiting for my family and friends to arrive. I don't have my suit on. My personal belongings are waiting in a cardboard box that my son said he'd carry to the car for me.

You see, today is my last day of work. In the past two years I've put in the time and effort to grow my network marketing business. It's to the point where I've replaced my income and no longer need a day job to provide for my family. It's a great day. I can't tell you how it feels. Hopefully you'll learn my lessons and do the same.

Well, I've gotta go. Melissa and the kids just pulled up ahead of James and the rest of the caravan.

Good luck, my friend. Keep your sights on your dreams and never look back. I can't wait until you're here with me. Signing off,

My Name is Dan, and I am Free.

+++++

NOTES

NOTES

We hope you've enjoyed Dan's story. If you did, please take a minute to leave a review on Amazon.

For information on business partnership go to http://contact.daviddelevante.com.

To take a 10-minute online health assessment and receive 3 free reports go to http://health.daviddelevante.com

For more information on this on-going series and author C. G. Cooper please visit http://www.CarlosCooper.com

www.ingramcontent.com/pod-product-compliance
Lightning Source LLC
Chambersburg PA
CBHW051815170526
45167CB00005B/2029